BOWLFULS OF BLUE

ALEXANDRA MCINTOSH

Copyright © 2021 by Alexandra Mcintosh

All Rights Reserved. No part of this book may be performed, recorded, used or reproduced in any manner whatsoever without the written consent of the author and the permission of the publisher except in the case of brief quotations embodied in critical articles and review.

An imprint of Assure Press Publishing & Consulting, LLC

www.assurepress.org

ASSURE PRESS

Publisher's Note: Assure Press books may be purchased for educational, business, or sales promotional use. For information please visit the website.

Bowlfuls of Blue/ Alexandra Mcintosh— 1st ed.

ISBN-13: 978-1-954573-04-8
eISBN-13: 978-1-954573-05-5
Library of Congress Control Number: 2021930013

ACKNOWLEDGMENTS

Earlier versions of the following poems first appeared in these publications. I'm extremely grateful to the journals' editors for their commitment to poetry, and the opportunity to share mine with the world.

Allegory Ridge: "Fluid Dynamics"

Milk and Cake Press, "My Grandmother's Funeral"

Red Flag Poetry: "The Names of Saints"

Raw Art Review: "The pond in front of the library," "Zubiri," "Constellation," "If We Must Make Judgements About What This All Means"

Broad River Review: "10,000 Things"

River River Journal: "Listening to Beethoven's Archduke Trio"

Penultimate Peanut Magazine: "Violent Engines"

Tiny Seed Literary Journal: "The Universe is a Loud Place"

Prometheus Dreaming Journal: "Heavy as It Is"

Griffel Magazine: "Paintings of Waterfowl"

My gratitude also extends to The Raw Art Review, Atlanta Review, Broad River Review, and The Tuxedo Project for the honor of various awards for poems from this collection.

CONTENTS

10,000 Things	1
The Names of Saints	2
The pond in front of the library	3
Fluid Dynamics	4
Constellation	5
Anxiety	6
Lately	7
Listening to Beethoven's Archduke Trio	8
Heavy as It Is	9
Paintings of Waterfowl	10
My Soul Rests in Little Pieces of Beauty	11
Daze	12
Park Street	13
Imago	14
That Wild Bird	15
The American Work Week	16
How Can We Be Sure?	17
Heart Murmur	18
Lines	19
I Wanted to Hold Your Hand at Evan's Funeral	20
Benjamin Button Must've Been in a Big Hurry	21
Bob Dylan Makes Me Miss You	22
Middle School Melodrama	23
Elaborate Love Apparatus	24
Another Poem About Love	25
Ellipses	26
Boda de Destino	27
What Art	28
Wandering Heavenly Bodies	29
Pinyon and Juniper	30
El Camino	31
Albergue	32
Saint Jean Pied de Port	33
We Carried This Tenderness With Us	34
Nocturne	35
Drink	36
The Day's Eye	37
The Sign	38

Nausea	39
Reasonable Distances	40
South of Cincinnati	41
Obsessive	42
Violent Engines	43
Mechanical Weathering	44
Missing the Forest	45
Kentucky River Longing	46
The Universe is a Loud Place	47
The Sound Factory	48
Portrait of My Grandfather as a Boy	49
Moon Drops	50
The Child Obscurely	51
Aquamarine	52
Golightly	53
My Grandmother's Funeral	54
Requiem: Mass for the Dead	55
Portrait of My Father's Grandfather	56
Fill the Valley	57
Two Birds	58
For Beauty	59
Recurring Dream	60
Lodge Lane	61
If We Must Make Judgements About What This All Means	62
Pray in Color	63
Benediction	64
About the Author	65

BOWLFULS OF BLUE

10,000 Things

I tried to stay awake for the meteor shower,
the Perseid Outburst dripping fire, searing
brackets across the sky. I fell asleep
beneath an off-white ceiling, a fan humming
circles, breathing coolness against my face
and hands. I once heard a man say, *God
is doing 10,000 wonderful things right now
and you're only aware of one.* I notice, though,
how the breeze from the fan lifts loose threads
from my grandmother's quilt, the streetlight
turning them gold. We must be underestimating.

The Names of Saints

The ones I remember: caramel-crested
fields of wheat along the highway,
Saint Jean, the sun, the smack
of diving boards, a full stomach,
my stuffed rabbit's ears, Saint Cecilia,
her blood collected on napkins,
Saint Theresa, the neighbor's daughter
toddler-dancing in the grass,
Saint Francis and his animals,
the cotton collar on a windbreaker
I hid under when it stormed, Saint Sebastian,
his body in a Roman sewer,
my dad's calloused hand, a lullaby
cassette tape my mom played before bed,
Saint Mary, orchids, chicory,
the squish of worms under rain boots,
my baby cousin smiling, Saint James
the Less, the wrinkles in the church carpet,
the pictures my brother drew
in hymnals to make me laugh,
Saint Joseph with hair like my grandpa
because they share a name.

The pond in front of the library

is dark green, unnatural green like the ponds
in front of big houses along the highway.
The water looks thick, more like jelly than water,
curdled by the flutter of duck feet under
shining duck bodies, water whipped like the butter
from milk on my great grandfather's farm,
the milk they'd churn into ice cream on Sundays.

My grandpa says he's never tasted ice cream so sweet,
not in his wife's pies, or the pastries from
the deli on fifth street, not in the blue-ribbon
shortcake at the church picnic. He says he worries
his memory is failing. We're sitting on the bench
watching the birds circle in the water
and I notice the lines fanning out
from the corners of his eyes match my own.

Fluid Dynamics

Rain on the concrete
swells like ocean waves,
or Great Lakes, or broken legs.
The river in the street
carries dogwood flowers
and cut grass
toward the sewer opening
where Grizzly spooked a raccoon
one morning on our walk.
I'm always pulling him
out of the street.
He likes to walk on the pavement,
white belly reflected in the water
like frost on a windshield,
like fog above backroads, like
smoke on the water or 70s rock
or dust on the record player
in my grandparent's house.

Constellation

The Big Dipper gathers bowlfuls of deep blue space
as it spins each year around Polaris. Seven stars
like the sisters I've always wanted: Alkaid, Mizar,
Alioth, Megrez, Phad, Merak, Dubhe. Who names
the stars? And who chose the sex of my brother?
To take my sister before her birth? My mom still
thinks of her, each year around Halloween, when
she would have been born. Maybe the movement
of our solar system doesn't matter,
doesn't amount to anything in our short lifetimes.
But we are moving, and it's lovely when stars move.

Anxiety

Copper colored, the snails in the garden
ooze out of rusty shells, hide beneath
the wooden edges of flowerbeds.

Last week I read Joe Parini's "Hunch,"
about that ancient *snail of thought*
that crawls over dirt into weeds,
dark pellets rolling up over the sticky
underbelly, hang off the slick shell.

He didn't mention how often robins,
sharp hooks at the end of their beaks,
assault the *snail*, swallowed instantly
past orange tongues, the curves of gut.
Or how, on a busy highway,
that fragile creature is so easily crushed.

Lately

I whisper into the sleeves of my jacket,
keep my head down in coffee shops.
The fingernails and eyelashes of infants
are impossibly small. I avoid eye contact
with strangers, with anyone, really—
the rods and cones that make up
our irises make me nauseous.

The neighbor's garden gnome stands under
the azaleas, grins smugly as I hurry in
from the car. Have I always been this delicate?
The skin on my elbows scrapes the blankets
as I turn over in my sleep. One day I tripped
over the dog in the kitchen, the smooth marble
counter catching the arc between
my eye and eyebrow. It swelled up,
turned purple. In the bathroom light I saw
needle-thin veins the color of mulberries
pulsing beneath the skin. The world seems
too big a place, anymore, for tiny vessels
like these, too big a place for Sunday dinners
and clover flower crowns.

Listening to Beethoven's Archduke Trio

The tall flame dances
above the oil lamp
from the monastery gift shop.
Blue-fired-clay crafted
like the circles and holes
in limestone cliffs along the river.
Did a monk make this?
Bright piano notes rise and fall,
bolstered by arcs of cello.
I'm reminded of a childhood game,
a circle of elementary schoolers
trying to keep a feather airborne
using just our breath. Giggling
into the middle, I lift my chin
so warm air catches the feather
by its threads, lofts it back
up toward the rafters.
Spinning river, leaping flame,
the eight-year-old laughing,
her breath enough
to keep the whole thing afloat.

Heavy as It Is

I can't hear it anymore— the creek behind
the elementary school parking lot—the veins
run so hot through my ears. Can't hear my
dad's voice or the lures rattling in his tackle box.
In grade school, the lot was painted with
the alphabet: Violet *A*, turquoise *L*, yellow *X*.
The *I* was missing. We looked for it all
school year, down on our bellies, hands against
the blacktop. Later, learned a deer died there,
hit by a car speeding around the building;
it washed away with animal blood and spit.

Paintings of Waterfowl

Rain against the earth's surfaces, a million
tiny percussions. If I couldn't have arms,
I'd want a duck beak, feather-layers
to tuck it into, warm as your down comforter.
A few rain-notes splash in the creek, drop
down rapids, sink in coolness towards
the ocean, the salty coastal birds. You
sit beside me. The field by the creek,
the pockets and folds of Appalachia
fill with the sound, like the ducks' eyes
when they open, filling with light.

My Soul Rests in Little Pieces of Beauty

A pileated woodpecker in the dogwood tree,
grey strokes of fog against the hillside, the creek,
gold field, red-winged blackbird in the chinquapin oak,
goldenrod in ditches along the highway,
milkweed and mountain mint, wild hyacinth
and mistflower, the coolness coaxing deer into clearings,
wild onion, marigold and phlox, the spider's web shiny
with dew. Slow rain. The bent grass at midnight.
The water rises, the river swells.

Daze

The shagbark maple is a tapestry
of green leaves, even this late in October.
All day, Grizzly chases a stub-tailed squirrel
around the yard. Bird songs remind me
of camping. Tuesday, I dreamt
I was swinging in a playground built
for adults. This morning I woke myself up
trying to keep the lead sticks in the
mechanical pencil of my dreams.

Park Street

My mom grew up on Park Street,
on Jello and John Denver, played Barbies
in cherry-wood houses on creek valley
hillsides dusted with wildflowers each spring,
watched neighbors smoke pipes
in the evenings, grey mist swirl toward
porch-roofs, seep into work clothes.
Goodnight hugs, face pressed into
her dad's cherry-tobacco coveralls,
sun-leathered lips against her forehead.

When I was young she coached swim team,
carried a clipboard at swim meets,
hand-wrote our events on note cards
the stroke-judges collected before each race.
She laughed as she taught us
to bite the corners off the relay cards—
one corner for each of us. *It's tradition,*
we'd tell the new kids. Whisper
good luck behind the diving blocks,
the tall lights above the pool collecting
moths like froth on top of a latte,
above the swim club near Park Street,
a bowl of light beneath the dark hills,
the quiet houses filled with cherry-wood.

Imago

In biological terms, imago *is the last stage in an insect's metamorphosis.*

Channel Five reports the number of cicadas as they hatch,
plays on loop a video of stained-glass wings opening
above thick abdomens. The pictures turn my stomach,
but I watch. As kids, my brother and his friends
chased me around the backyard holding the bugs.
I dodged swing sets, climbed the neighbor's pitch pine
avoiding the exoskeletons that lined the tree's limbs.

The boys inside, I crawled down from the tree,
scratched sap off my fingers, and collected the bodies.
I was old enough to know I should crush them,
missing wings and wounded torsos, but left them writhing
in piles under the pine tree for the neighbor's cat.

That Wild Bird

From the bridge behind the office park
I saw a blue heron. The line of trees,
the undergrowth, the creek
littered with plastic bottles.
Dark feet in the stream,
he sidled over limestone ledges
further, further until he rounded
a bend and was out of sight.

The American Work Week

In dreams, I shop for notebooks
like I shop for rugs, on giant hangers
swinging like the poster racks at K-mart
when I was a kid, when grade school
projector-slides glowed like sunsets
on drywall. I'm in the university library
now, and I can barely keep my eyes open.
I wonder if people notice. Maybe
they think I'm focused, believe the rumor
I started that all poets meditate.

How Can We Be Sure?

The sun, caught in the locust tree,
brightens the city windows, the skyline.
Predisposed to kiss softly and hold hands,
we sit quietly in the garden, season our food,
collect rocks, buy prints of Picasso's, take videos
of puppies, pick wildflowers and nicknames.
How can we be sure that our existence amounts
to nothing more than survival, than climbing
out of the primordial goo at the beginning
of the world, staying close to the ground
as our planetary orb spins faster and faster?

Heart Murmur

My dog leans heavily against my legs,
I bend down to hug him. I'm not sure
if he understands mirrors, but he whines
at my reflection and wags his tail.
Some nights I wake to the thought
that Grizzly could die young. I reach out,
feel him breathing, soft body curled
into the larger curve of mine.
He sleeps while I count the pads of his feet,
the joints of his tail, two ears, the whiskers
behind his nose. I never understood,
when I was young, why couples hold hands
at the grocery or kiss over Chinese food.
Now I leave parties early, watch
his silhouette fill the window.

Lines

It takes a lot of time in the sun to stay
tan through the winter. It's usually
just men who work construction, their
arm and neck tans stopping abruptly
at t-shirt edges. Dylan had one of
those tans when I saw him at a
concert last summer. There are some
people we want who we'll never have.
I wanted to trace the olive circle
around his bicep with my finger, to
kiss the golden ring around his neck.

I Wanted to Hold Your Hand at Evan's Funeral

Everyone's head was bowed and you
were so close. Once when the grass
was wet and I couldn't find my shoes,
you gave me a piggy-back ride, laughed,
held my hands against your heart.

I can't look you in the eyes for long,
afraid you'll notice my face soften
when you speak. When you're driving
I watch your eyelashes sway over
your eyes, the blue color of morning,
10 am before the fog burns off.

Your upper lip curves like the birds I drew
above beaches in middle school notebooks.
The Beach Boys tape I found at Goodwill
turns over in the tape deck, and I fold
my arms to hide the glowing in my chest.

Benjamin Button Must've Been in a Big Hurry

The rain was a symphony, puppy, and the symphony was a thunderstorm. I've always thought it would be nice to call a boyfriend *puppy*, but saying it out loud sounds silly. Maybe I could call a baby *puppy*, maybe a dog. Sitting in the balcony of Music Hall, the stage lights look like roses, gold shining on bald heads and seat backs where the players sit straight up. I've always admired good posture. The old man next to me leaned over after the third opus (a funny word) to tell his wife that the woman in front of them was sleeping. They laughed together, holding hands. I wonder if she calls him puppy. Anyway, the music was thunderously loud, louder than normal, and I watched the stage-hands run around nervous. The old people in the audience—it's mostly old people—turned down their hearing aids but didn't seem to mind otherwise. I'm getting too young for this.

Bob Dylan Makes Me Miss You

And station wagons, film cameras
and the water fountain where we stopped
with Grizzly when he was a puppy.
He missed you, too, I think,
when we passed it today on our way to the park.
The wind blew his ears back like
a dog food commercial. You would've loved that.
The whole way a teenager across the street
parallel to us with a Bluetooth speaker
played vaguely familiar pop music, the kind
we both hate. (Me and you, not me and Grizzly.
He'll listen to anything.) It's music that makes
me think of you most often, old music. And
the sound of a tape flipping over in a tape deck.

The mixtape you gave me for Christmas
is in my desk drawer because my car
only has a slot for CDs. It doesn't make me sad
to see it, when I open the drawer to grab a post-it,
but it does make me think of you, of the first time
you kissed me, after the concert while
we sobered up. It doesn't feel sad to miss you
anymore, it's just there sometimes,
like the quiet at the end of a track.

Middle School Melodrama

On my nightstand: a plastic flower in a little vase
with plastic beads for soil. Before prayers and after lights-out
I'd lift a soil-bead between my thumb and index finger,
a delicate oval catching light through the curtain. Quietly,
like a secret, I'd place the brown gem on the windowsill.
A tiny sacrament, a testament to my patience. One more day
of loving Caleb. One more day of him not knowing.
And please, Lord, let Caleb like me back. Amen.

I don't remember when I stopped adding beads to the pile,
when I swept the fake dirt into my pink trash can.
But yesterday on the porch of my parents' house,
I saw Caleb on a run; down the hill and out of sight
while the white petals on the Bradford pear trees glistened.
The last traces of morning rain caught in sunlight,
vaporized by that glorious mystery called evaporation.

Elaborate Love Apparatus

Thomas Merton, monk and hermit, fell in love
with his nurse. In high school, my grandma
mistook her future husband's speech impediment
for an exotic accent. All the time, everywhere
people are falling in love. In 7th grade Ryan smiled,
nudged me with his elbow like my big brother does.
Daniel drove a Volkswagen, the silver finish
reflected the trees above Route 8. Later,
my first kisses were ocean waves. Rush after rush
of lace over ankles, smile creases and strong shoulders.
Boxes of tears, a hill on Bellevue Street,
the body-hurt of unanswered love.

Honey, what more could I want? The sky, summer wind,
a storm, purple light. Pollen-drunk bumblebees
over blossoms. What more could I want, having this:
a house under sycamores and people to love.
Sun in my eyelashes and Grizzly. And books,
warm socks, and a space heater. The trails
behind the Monastery opening up to show the stars.

Another Poem About Love

Against a navy darkness, she
holds her son. Waiting for the school bus
in a lawn chair on the driveway, she speaks
softly, secret words. Mourning doves,
bare branches overhead. Snuggled
warm in her lap, his winter coat
and clumsy gloves keep out the cold.

Ellipses

It rained on the lake in July, the little window
by my houseboat bunk cast a dull light on my pillow
each morning. The smooth water puckered,
valleyed and peaked, small drops like happy
tears or the diamonds on the engagement ring
my brother bought in May. *Satellites,* he told me,
thousands of satellites, maybe more, their metal bodies
glissade along orbital paths. It's midday now,
the sun hangs over the oak tree so I can't see them,
but I feel them gilding circles around the earth.

Boda de Destino

My brother played Elton John on their first date,
the old piano in the Green Kayak on the Ohio River.
Lauren's hands are in his now, "Somebody to Love"
plays on speaker. This place, Playa del Carmen,
the Yucatan Peninsula, hundreds of thousands,
millions of years. Sand is made, it moves
along beaches. Love goes with it. Out of all,
find another. Waves carry broken coral,
soft against us as we swim, dive under to pull
each other's feet, like Josh did when we were kids.

What Art

—to wake at midnight, lumber downstairs
stop at the fridge, sit at the table
the overhead lamp wicked bright,
to eat the party leftovers
turn out the light, return to bed.

Wandering Heavenly Bodies

The field along Memorial is lined with redbuds.
Herds of deer graze there, mornings and evenings.
In spring, translucent petals lift from the trees
and float across the road, land on the sidewalk,
on windshields, on the bloated bodies of roadkill.

In Florida, our hotel was right on the water.
We followed the boardwalk between sand dunes,
left our shoes in a pile, stumbled toward the waves
to look up at the stars. Barefoot, the sand beneath us.
The planets enormous, not tiny as they appear,
wander along their celestial spheres.

Pinyon and Juniper

Once in Utah I set up my tent in a narrow gulch,
rock wall on one side, Dead Man's Creek on the other.
The ground was embroidered with cacti, little
as the ones filling pots at my aunt's house.
In the morning, tiny spikes caught the wool
of my socks. The creek's rhythm padded my stumbling,
my hurried movements through the canyon's dawn,
before the sun rose and lit the walls golden.

El Camino

Spanish grasses part around our hips. Sheep,
sticky with brambles, glance up from grazing,
creek pools reflect shepherd-shapes, hazy
across plains. Big dogs follow the herds,
hedge them in on mountains, bed down
with them at dusk. Bracken ferns catch
raindrops, and falcons wheel along cliff edges.

Albergue

The hosts, an elderly couple, met us at the gate with Spanish greetings and umbrellas, collected us into the cathedral basement. They served coffee in bowls when the mugs ran out, cleaned around piles of guidebooks, smiled as we studied route plans and bandaged feet. In the main room, a mandolin was snuggled behind cleaning supplies, left by a pilgrim whose load was too heavy. When he learned I could play, the old man stood on a chair to reach it. With an E string broken and others out of tune, I played a hymn. I had no room in my pack for the mandolin, but I carried the song with me, over hills and mountain passes, through valleys and villages. It harmonized with rivers and birds, with pub crowds and city traffic. On nights I couldn't sleep, I heard it mix with the pilgrim snores rising from the bunks around me, the breathing and rustling of bodies turning beneath their covers.

Saint Jean Pied de Port

There's a wild horse on the mountain,
its mane whips around in the wind.
Sheep up that high wear bells, gusts
swing their music side to side, up
and down. The air below is warmer,
beneath the storm; we're wearing shorts.
Hail stings our legs, we huddle under trees,
let it pass. Clouds roll up the mountain,
hide the sheep like puffs of smoke
when a magician disappears. One cloud
breaks and a man carrying a bicycle
walks out, must have carried it the whole
way up. Storms are funny, the things
they hide, the things they reveal.

We Carried This Tenderness With Us

The donkey in Zubiri seemed
to know us, greeted us gently like
an old dog. We took turns wrapping
our arms around his neck, the full
weight of his head on our shoulders,
a blessing like the words the sisters
had spoken in Roncesvalles. We left him
in the field, muzzle on a stone fence,
the path's dust staining our ankles.

Nocturne

I couldn't sleep in Spain,
so I sat in courtyards and dreamt.
Narrow streets carried voices
around the cities' sharp turns.
Pubs were open late, groups
of old men sat outside for centuries.
Ornate churches, squares filled
with benches, fountains where
people used to collect water,
dogs lapping between moons.
The old men spoke Spanish,
but the night and the cities
spoke languages I understood.

Drink

In the Rocky Mountains, behind the shadow
of the Grand Tetons, two moose—
a mother and calf— bent to take a drink.
I saw them from the boulder by the creek,
a pool where the stream dropped
half a foot on its way down, down from
the mountain pass into the autumn valley.
They lifted their heads from shoulder-high bushes,
and startled me. A cool gust caught my hair,
mingled with pine, huckleberry, fir.
My empty water bottles and iodine,
their hooves, muzzles dripping
(whole galaxies in each drop) above
the mountain's crumbling, changing, growth.

The Day's Eye

Chicory flowers tangled fences
by my first apartment, twisted
through my neighbor's lawn.
One day, at lunchtime, the blue
flowers were missing. Eaten,
I figured, by deer, or plucked by kids.
Later, I found that chicory closes
around noon when sunshine pulls
moisture from the plant's spikey
edges. Daisy petals, too, open with
the sun, close at night. Slender ovals
like eyelashes catch the light, rest.
Victorians called daisies *the eyes
of the day.* The world is watchful.

The Sign

The pink speckled neck of a sidewalk pigeon stretches and shrinks, rough claws scrape violet cement, tinted beneath an overcast afternoon. The neck expands and contracts, falls into sync with the blinking crosswalk light, the signal chanting *walk now, walk now* in a woman's electronic voice. Across the street, the elderly man who drags a park chair to the curb each day and watches traffic, straightens his back, observing the synchronization. I raise my hand, call out to him, but my voice is carried up High Street, away from the man, away from the pigeon, away.

Nausea

The vastness of space exposes us.
A friend in college thought deeply
about the galaxy and threw up.

Our bodies rebuild themselves
every seven years; the membranes
between organs painted over
like the roads' yellow lines.

The river moves constantly.
I visit Lock 7 each April,
high water pummels driftwood
against stone columns.

All the world is static and flow, chaos
and constancy. How are we to cope?

Reasonable Distances

At Kentucky's State Fair, children watch rabbits,
stick fingers into cages. They laugh and coo,
call the hulking bodies of pigs closer, scratch
the trembling ears of goats. The animals back into
metal corners, whiskers show the quickness of breath.
Trust us, children plead, *we won't hurt you.*
And they don't, they wouldn't. But behind them
adults exchange money, swap recipes for Burgoo.

South of Cincinnati

Bluegrass rolls into the Ohio River.
Whispers of coal country;
factories digested the hills' dark organs.
Old skeletons, windowless ghosts
adorn the farmland, the waterways.

Obsessive
Compulsive
Disorder

                          compartmentalizes
my thinking
into left
                       and right

bad
                      and good.
                      The sunlight in prisms
                              on the water glass,
the shadows
and oil beneath
                      shining
slick cars.
                      Silence.

The noise
                      of the creek
                            falling over limestone
                            ledges,
                      the order of thought
the dark cloud
around the edges
of words.

Violent Engines

I found a baby goldfinch, a fledgling,
hopping like the stuffed chick in my Easter basket
in third grade, a wind-up thing. The road was busy,
kids played by the middle school, so I ushered
the squeaking creature into an alcove formed
by the roots of an oak tree, whispered to it
like I would my dog, explained in English—
the only language I have— that I wasn't leaving it
alone, that its mom would be back when I left.

It rained that night, lights from the school shone
on the wet street and I thought of the goldfinch.
Of its mother foraging for food, carrying it back
in her belly. Of the deer who laid her fawn under
the oak tree one summer, returned each night
until it could follow. I thought of the tender spot
on my thigh that I don't remember bruising, and all
the wounds my body heals without my knowledge.

Mechanical Weathering

National Geographic shows a time lapse
of a birch tree growing through concrete
and I feel it in my throat. Root fibers stretch
like feathers between my vocal chords,
the cortex pulses where my chest cavity
meets my neck. I feel it beating there
above my actual heart, the pressure in my
esophagus. It would be nice to tell you this
is how my anxiety feels, to call this growth
my OCD. I try and speak, it branches into
my belly, forms a burl above my right eye.
The mass bobs up and down as I blink and
no one notices. I glance up to watch it,
peripherally, stop in the middle of my
sentences, pretend it's an eyelash. Try to
refute the grotesque way it blocks the light.

Missing the Forest

I pass a semi on the highway— *Make Your Land
More Productive* in bold green brushstrokes.
The square frame slaps the air, a groaning *woosh*,
metallic-gasoline-scent through my open window.

Behind it, hills fresh with wildflowers
roll toward the horizon, the Kentucky River
hums, and families of deer stop to drink.

Kentucky River Longing

The biology professor found the fish,
its sharp teeth caught in the woven plastic of the net.
I took its slender body in my bare hands.
The gar's prehistoric organs secreted sticky
river-water-turned-slime. It coated my fingers,
pooled in the creases of my palms. Long after
I placed the fish back in the shallow water,
it stuck with me—the smell, the feel of muscles
under slime and speckled skin—bright in my mind
like the glare of the river on a day in August.

The Universe is a Loud Place

NASA has recorded the interactions of electromagnetic particles from solar wind, ionosphere, and planetary magnetosphere, and translated these vibrations into sound waves.

Lie on your back
on the front porch,
look up at the sky,
at the white gutter,

up at the wooden ceiling,
the hanging pots heavy
with ferns. Look up
at the cumulus clouds,

their flat undersides
and cotton-ball tops.
Look at the air
above your house,

picture the multitudes
of electromagnetic waves
wiggling above you from
radio towers and cellphones,

microwaves and stereos.
Consider the infrared light
warming the pavement,
the neighbor's sleeping dog;

the visible light of the sun,
streetlights at dusk;
the ultraviolet, x-ray, gamma
waves flashing across galaxies.

Lie on your back and
tell me you feel them,
their buzzing and whirling,
their constant motion.

The Sound Factory

Grizzly stayed inside yesterday, the rain heavy
on the windows. Today he laid in the flower bed,
all morning despite the cold. My grandpa tells me
often about cold mornings on the farm growing up.
My hands are chapped already from winter. I wish
I could have known him as a boy, reckless,
hot-tempered. The crickets in the creek bed behind
the farmhouse, his family gathered around the radio.
My grandpa clears his throat before he speaks.
Tomorrow will be cold again, the snow-turned-
ice still frozen on the back deck. When do words
become music? Language buzzing through airwaves,
caught singing by antennas and ear cartilage.
Tomorrow, I'll write all day, my legs warmed
by the space heater humming beneath my desk.

Portrait of My Grandfather as a Boy

In childhood, his brothers carried him down
from their house on the bluff, carried him down
the muddy slopes of grass, the tree roots winding
like black snakes curled up in the August sun,
down to the water lapping against the slimy bank.
Laughing, they'd throw him in, the splash speckling
their tan chests and faces, the wrinkles around their eyes.
Gasping and spitting, he'd surface, paddle toward them,
toward the brown bank, where the green water
rocked against the mud. It was a game they played,
carrying the littlest boy to the water, him fighting
and smiling. He liked the game, the closeness
of their bodies as they paraded under the sycamores,
the cool shock of water, the splashing towards shore.
He liked climbing out of the river, muddy hands pulling
him onto the bank, liked chasing his brothers around,
their bodies shiny from the water droplets.

But most of all he liked the quiet, the moment beneath
the water after the splash, the slow movements
of his body towards the muddy floor of the river,
the squish of mud through his toes, and the quick sliding
back up towards the surface, up towards the air,
towards the sycamores, and the laughing of his brothers.

Moon Drops

Tuesday, I cut basil, fry potatoes. A long walk, bright
quarter moon, the dark circle behind it. Light
from the city melts through park tree silhouettes,
the way my grandfather butters toast, smooths the liquid
into bread pores. Crumbs fall onto his plate, bounce
onto our napkins. Somehow there are always crumbs
in his coffee. He lifts his mug to take a drink, the steam
fogs up his glasses so he squints at me across the table.

The Child Obscurely

We climbed the water tower, the tall ladder
through Northern Kentucky darkness,
humidity, insect songs. Orange cigarettes
at the top, ashes flicked over, turn grey
in the breeze, then black, lost in the space
between sky and ground. Below us
a train lit up the trees like lampshades.

I heard a story once about a man visiting
who climbed the tower during a storm.
He was almost at the top when lightning
struck, brightening the water in the tank,
racing down the ladder and through the man.
I don't know how long he was up there,
how he got down. But he moved into town
after that, moved with his whole family
and their three dogs. I wonder
if that's how most people find home—
a bolt of lightning in a thunderstorm?
For me it was quieter, the careful breaths
of my brother as he climbed ahead of me.

Aquamarine

Born in March, my mom wears the gemstone
around her neck every day, unwinds
the chain from its heap on her jewelry box,
holds it up in window light to find the clasp,
drapes it around the olive curve of skin
below her ponytail, remakes its circle.

Golightly

The antique file cabinet by my bedroom window
still holds my great aunt's divider tabs: *current medical,*
museum exhibits, symphony, auto sale. The moon's
rarely visible from this window, but the street lamp
lights the curtains. My great aunt never married,
spent her life on airplanes and runways.
When I can't sleep I trace moon phases in my mind:
full, waxing, first quarter. I heard the things
they called her, brittle words. Aunt Mae would laugh,
adjust her scarf. In Mexico, the crescent moon hung
all day over the turquoise water, white streaks
of sandbars like the ivory comb on her dresser.
Soft things need soft language to match.

My Grandmother's Funeral

At the memorial service the light draws diamonds,
salmon-colored and sparkling,
on my folded hands. Hers are cold now,
across her chest, thin-skinned,
translucent like Bible pages,
reflected on the shiny surface of the coffin lid.

My grandfather sits beside me,
yellow fingers in his lap, head bowed.
He told me once, laughing, of his drunk wife
hemming his pants, sewing one leg
two inches shorter than the other.
Her face reddened, she smacked his hand,
smiled when he grabbed hers.
I did no such thing, in her teacher voice.

Driving home: the stereo buzz, raindrops
on the wind-shield pulsate, pool on the hood,
drop like eyelashes flicked off finger tips,
the oil-soaked street, water over blacktop,
dirt underneath, the wheels' distinctive *shhhhh*.

Will my hands be seen one day
in the mirror of a coffin, by great grandchildren?
And the skin on my fingers— will it shine?

Requiem: Mass for the Dead

Incense expands, smoking as it burns
up toward the cathedral's corners,
stained-glass, dust, faded saints.
Above the ashes of prayer candles,
the round shoulders and faces in pews,
rays of sunlight catch the smoke in columns.
The choir exhales— decrescendo.

Portrait of My Father's Grandfather

Smiling, he holds a catfish, glassy body reflected
in dark water, riffles, and glares. Grass blades
speckle the white field by the river, chunks of ice
break off from the bank. The clock
in the front room and a brass wind chime
swing against cold air to mark the time.
Between *where have you been* and *get out*—
Build. Roll. Change. The river will speak for itself
if you let it. Change, change, change.

Fill the Valley

A cardinal on the phone line broadcasts
its usual call. A guy I knew could whistle
their song and draw them in from the woods,
a pair. Vivid male, tan mate. They'd stand
on swaying branches, and tilt their necks
robotically. I could have watched for hours
but they caught on quick, followed each other
back into the woods, down the hill to the
sycamores, their white branches over the river.

Two Birds

Looking up from the fire I see them, cardinals,
in the neighbor's tree, the highest branches.
They seem to be watching the sky like I am.
They're facing that way, watching the clouds
from the west where the sun will soon set.

For Beauty

From now on, in place of "beauty,"
I will say "*!%#." Those are just symbols, too,
aren't they? I've grown so accustomed
to reading I'd forgotten these words are symbols,
drawings. I'd forgotten, too, that we're members
of families, trees in a forest. That membership
gives us weight, keeps us from floating away.
That humanity, history, memory give shape
to beauty. To *!%#. That light, dim as it seems,
makes art visible. Beautiful. *!%#ful.

Recurring Dream

I'm screaming, "art!" Running around
my parents' basement looking for the C & S Brand
suet birdfeed, the kind my dad swears by—
the birds love it— and I'm screaming, "art!"

They hung a metal feeder from the dogwood tree,
one of the thin branches over the sidewalk,
thought it'd be safe from the squirrels— it wasn't.

In my dream, the birdfeed is love and the cage is my heart.
The squirrels dangle by their back feet,
reach long fingers through the green wire,
knock the feed loose, cover the grass
with cylinders of crushed suet, mealworm,
peanut flour, so the birds gather in large groups.
And love, too. Love leaves us empty.

Lodge Lane

A sidewalk bridges the valley behind Woodland
Place. Leaves are falling and the back door
of the custom frame shop smacks shut. Deer under
the black walnut tree barely notice, the edges
of their ears twitch slightly, noses dig into the grass.
They eat the walnuts, lemony green shells break
softly, decorate the ground like candy wrappers.
I've never eaten a walnut in the wild. I stop
on the sidewalk, mist hangs like a question
over the grass. I know every street in this town,
the hilltops and porches best for sunsets.

If We Must Make Judgements About What This All Means

You said it feels presumptuous
even to be alive and conscious,
that it's arrogant
to believe in a divine kindness.
That faith, like pavement,
is eventually eaten up by the wilderness,
crumbled.

But my faith isn't concrete;
it's wild flowers.
Violets and black-eyed susan,
mountain laurel and bluebells.
Slender greenery rips through driveways,
tears up sidewalks.
I would rather err on the side of hope,
the divine melody that spins the earth
around the sun and knit our cells together
in the dampness of the womb.
The emerald river hops over pebbles,
monsoons replenish the soil,
lavender blankets hillsides,
and a solar ball of fire dances
colorfully in morning rain.

Instead of convincing ourselves
that none of this matters,
why not surrender to the wind,
the strong tide, the warm sun,
the great wonder of being?

Pray in Color

Kentucky River palisades   cabin porch rocking chair
old dog blind as love asleep at my feet   guitar music
fire smell   fresh-baked   coffee after dinner

Yucatan blue   beach sand   bedrock   feldspar
the sea creatures' tough shells   a larimar ring
my mother gave me   her laughter

sun on the wall   Mary Oliver   Rumi
Hafiz   Wendell Berry   the words of Jesus
Annie Dillard   Tolkien   Coleridge

knit blankets   pink foxgloves painted
on cloth Bibles   Lasagna on Christmas   sauerkraut
in pots on New Year's   my grandmother's leather belt

spider web   in the trees' highest branches   Kentucky
autumn   Grizzly chasing deer through underbrush
honeysuckle   the owl we saw last spring

these things have taught me to pray

Benediction

When mist settles,
swollen leaves pad the earth
like pages in a wet book.
The whole country is baptized.
Walk in the morning
and wonder if water
seeps up from the earth
or soaks down from the sky.

ABOUT THE AUTHOR

Alexandra McIntosh lives and writes in Kentucky, her favorite place in the world. She received her B.A. from Asbury University, her M.A. in English from Northern Kentucky University, and her MFA in Poetry from Miami University. Her writing explores memory, both personal and communal, and its connection to the natural world. She is currently teaching college English and working on her next book: a memoir about family stories and the landscapes they create. Her poetry and creative nonfiction can be found in publications including *Sad Girls Club*, *Milk and Cake Press*, *Raw Art Review*, and *Griffel Magazine*. You can find links to her publications and pictures of her dog on her website AlexandraMcIntosh.com.

  facebook.com/alexandra.mcintosh.71216
  twitter.com/realalexmac
  instagram.com/the_real_alexmac